Pennsylvania Wildlife Tails

A Game Warden's Notebook

By

William Wasserman

William Wasserman

Illustrations

By

Dana Twigg

Pennsylvania Wildlife Tails
A Game Warden's Notebook

By
William Wasserman

Illustrations
By
Dana Twigg

Other books by William Wasserman
The Best of It's a Wild Life
Published by The New Age-Examiner
P.O. Box 59, Tunkhannock, PA 18657

ISBN 0-9718907-0-6

*For my wife, Marianne,
who has always had
a great sense of humor*

Introduction

Having spent more than half my life working as a Pennsylvania wildlife conservation officer, I've learned one indisputable fact about animals: whenever you tell someone that a wild critter won't behave (or misbehave for that matter) in a certain way, you're bound to be made a fool of.

Our furred and feathered friends have been surprising me with their antics for close to three decades now, and I thought it high time to share some of these stories with other folks who love the outdoors. I wrote this book for people who treasure wild birds and wild animals, and who enjoy the feeling of wonder and laughter that ordinary animals can evoke when they act in extraordinary ways.

Herein you will find 48 of the most unusual, comical, amazing and absurd stories I've ever heard on the subject of people and animals. Some will make you laugh, others may astonish you…but be assured, dear reader, every one is true!

And he went back through the Wet Wild Woods, waving his wild tail and walking by his wild lone. But he never told anybody.

Rudyard Kipling

Whooo's Calling

Late one evening my wife and I were sitting on the porch when our neighbor's telephone began ringing. It made a soft, trilling sound; and with each ring, a distant screech owl would call back with its own haunting whinny. My wife remarked that it was the first time she had ever heard an owl answer a phone.

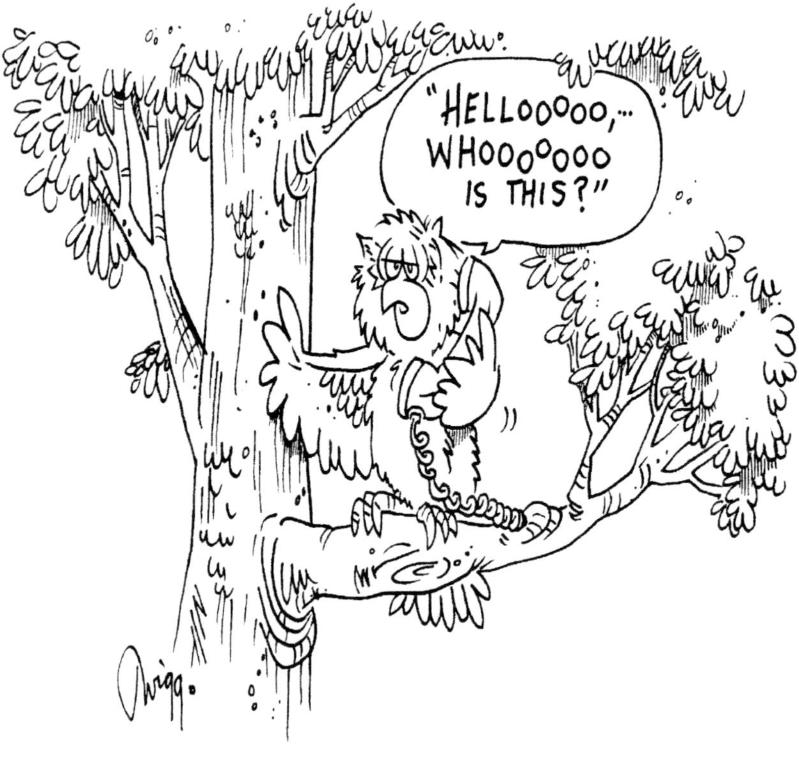
"HELLOOOOO,...
WHOOOOOOO
IS THIS?"
Twigg

It's all in the Wrist

Brenda Charles stopped her car and stared in comic disbelief as a porcupine shambled blindly along the berm, its head wedged firmly inside an empty bean can. She wanted to help the critter but didn't want to be injured by its sharp quills. Luckily, her neighbor happened by and knew exactly what to do. Lifting the can with both hands, he shook it until the porcupine plopped out. Brenda said some folks can really drain a can of porc 'n beans in a hurry!

"HA HA... STUCK YOUR NOSE WHERE IT DIDN'T BELONG AGAIN HUH, PORC?"
BEANS
Quiggo

Nice Day for A Ride

I was driving along a congested highway one day when the truck ahead of me stopped for a groundhog in the middle of the road. As it continued on, the groundhog seemed to have disappeared. But I soon saw the critter balancing itself on the truck's rear axle. Perhaps he simply wanted to hitch a ride to greener pastures.

Not so Wily

While hunkered down in camouflage, hunting turkeys, Jerry Evans had two fine gobblers strutting toward him when a coyote suddenly appeared from out of nowhere and snatched one of his plastic decoys. The two *real* turkeys took off before the coyote realized his mistake...too late, of course, for Jerry or the coyote to enjoy a turkey dinner.

Counteraction

Gary Cobb saw a large bobcat moving stealthily toward the dark forest at the end of his property. Suddenly a doe stormed from the shadows, charged for the bobcat, and sent it scurrying. The feisty deer then bolted back into the forest and reappeared with twin fawns.

Doggone!

When Rod Azar taught his Golden Retriever, Turk to pad into the kitchen and fetch a can of soda, he became the envy of all his friends. But it appears Rod may have trained his dog a little too thoroughly because whenever they go hunting, the accommodating retriever scampers about fetching every discarded can in the countryside! It's getting so bad, Rod is thinking about bringing a trash container along on their next hunt.

The Music Police

When my daughter walked into my office and asked if she could play her clarinet for me, I happily agreed. Little Sarah was just learning, and although she wanted to perform a soothing melody, her notes came out choppy and strained.

Suddenly my police scanner came alive. Responding to some distant, inaudible transmission, a voice blurted, *"Try again, you're breaking up!"*

Sarah put down her clarinet and gazed at me in disbelief. "Daddy!" she exclaimed. "Can they hear me?"

A Kodak Moment

While hiking along a sparkling stream, I noticed a small black object lying on the bank. Stepping closer, I discovered someone had taken a scenic photograph and then carelessly dropped the negative where he'd stood!

Had a Bellyful

A sportsman I know checked the stomach contents of 8 American mergansers harvested by friends, and was surprised to find they had swallowed a combined total of 16 walleyes and one bass. The average length of each fish stretched between 6 and 12 inches!

Maternal Instinct

Stacy Matiskella wondered what was knocking over her birdbath every day. Then one morning she spotted a doe tipping the birdbath with its head so her fawns could lap the spilled water from the ground.

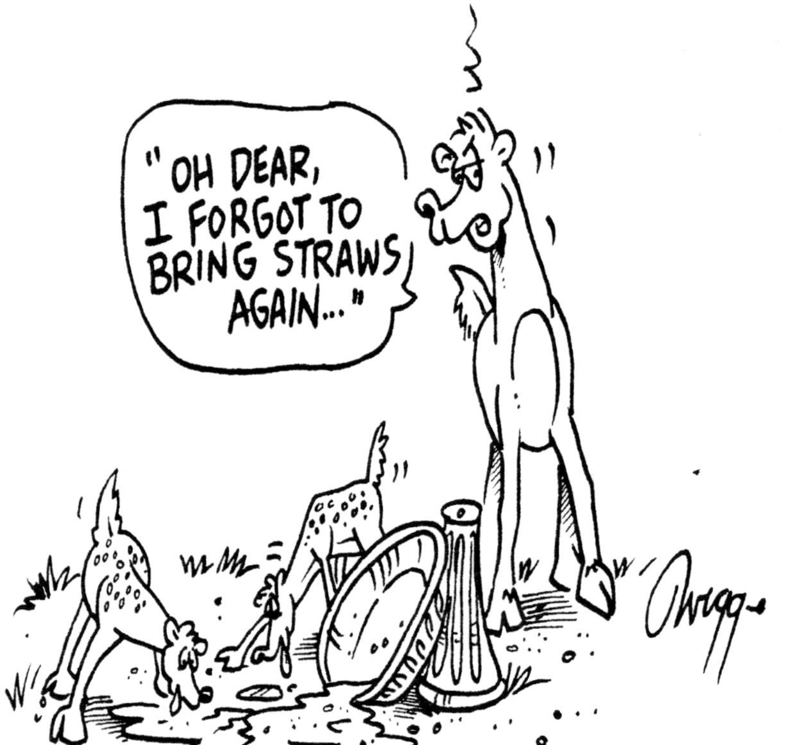
"OH DEAR, I FORGOT TO BRING STRAWS AGAIN..."
Owigg

Burglar Bunny

While mowing, I spooked a young rabbit, which darted into my open garage and hid under some heavy equipment. I left the garage door open figuring it would soon leave, but weeks later, I saw the same rabbit hiding among dozens of flowers my wife had stored inside the garage. The voracious bunny had eaten half of them! Finding food and shelter, it apparently had never left. I managed to catch the rabbit and get it out of the garage...but now *I'm* in the doghouse!

Father Knows Best

Ralph Anderson was out for a walk when he stumbled upon one of the 60 quail he'd released into the wild. It was a male sitting on 15 eggs. Three weeks later Ralph saw the same quail trailed by 13 poults! It looked like he was enjoying his role as a stay-at-home dad.

LISTEN KIDS, YOUR MOM IS WORKING. YOU'RE JUST GOING TO HAVE TO HANG WITH ME UNTIL YOU'RE OLDER...
Wiggins

On the Ball

When game warden Randy Shoup heard that a grocery clerk had been bragging about her husband shooting an eagle, he launched a full-scale investigation. Randy soon discovered that golden and bald eagles aren't the only variety in Pennsylvania. A third and equally rare eagle can also be found. Its habitat is restricted to country clubs, and it is shot, from time to time by skilled golfers. They call it two under par.

Teamwork

A mother rabbit dug a nest in my lawn, lining it with grass and belly fur, then raised her three nurslings there. After the tiny rabbits outgrew it and moved on, a pair of tree swallows transported the abandoned nest, piece by piece, into a nearby birdhouse. Consequently, the swallows successfully raised three fledglings in a nest built by birds, with material provided by a rabbit, inside a house produced by a man. Now that's what I call cooperation!

Treed

John Gabries was deer hunting when he happened upon a beaver trapped by the tree it had just cut down. The trunk had landed firmly upon its tail, and the creature was doomed to a death by predators or starvation.

Working feverishly, John gathered rocks for a fulcrum and pulled a stout branch from the beaver's dam to pry the giant rodent free.

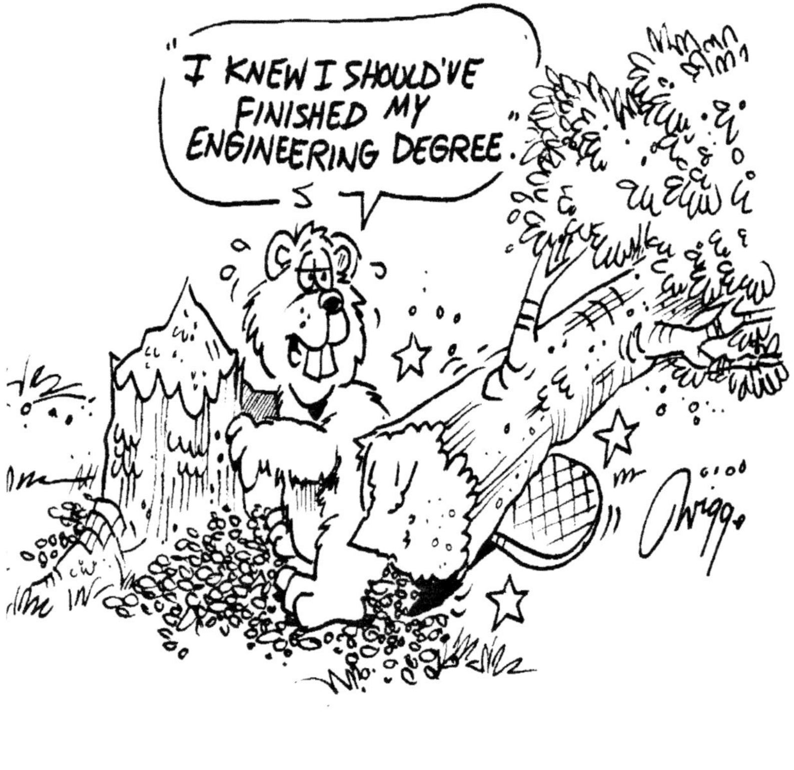
"I KNEW I SHOULD'VE FINISHED MY ENGINEERING DEGREE."
Twigg

Buon Appetite

Driving through suburban Philadelphia, Deputy Game Warden Tom Scarpello watched an osprey plummet into a pond surrounded by shopping malls, and arise with a small gold carp. Osprey sightings are rare throughout Pennsylvania but especially unusual in metropolitan areas. Tom thinks the advertisement for seafood at a nearby restaurant attracted the fishhawk.

Tricked!

One dark, October night, deputy warden Dick Zika received a report of people shining lights on deer and shooting at them. He jumped in his patrol car and rushed to the location; but to his surprise, the alleged spotlights turned out to be headlights from a tractor pulling a wagonload of children! The "gunshots" were merely air cannons used to intensify their spooky Halloween outing.

Common Scents

When a woman called me to complain about skunks stinking up the neighborhood, I tried to calm her, explaining that skunks do a lot of good by eating mice and small insects. She thought about this for a moment, then said, "You know...I think they might discourage prowlers too!" It sure made my argument feeble in comparison.

Dining by Candlelight

Doug Possinger sees a screech owl perched on a street lamp by his house every night. The light provides a smorgasbord of flying insects, and the owl doesn't have to lift a wing to catch them! Doug says he now knows how the adage, "wise old owl" came about.

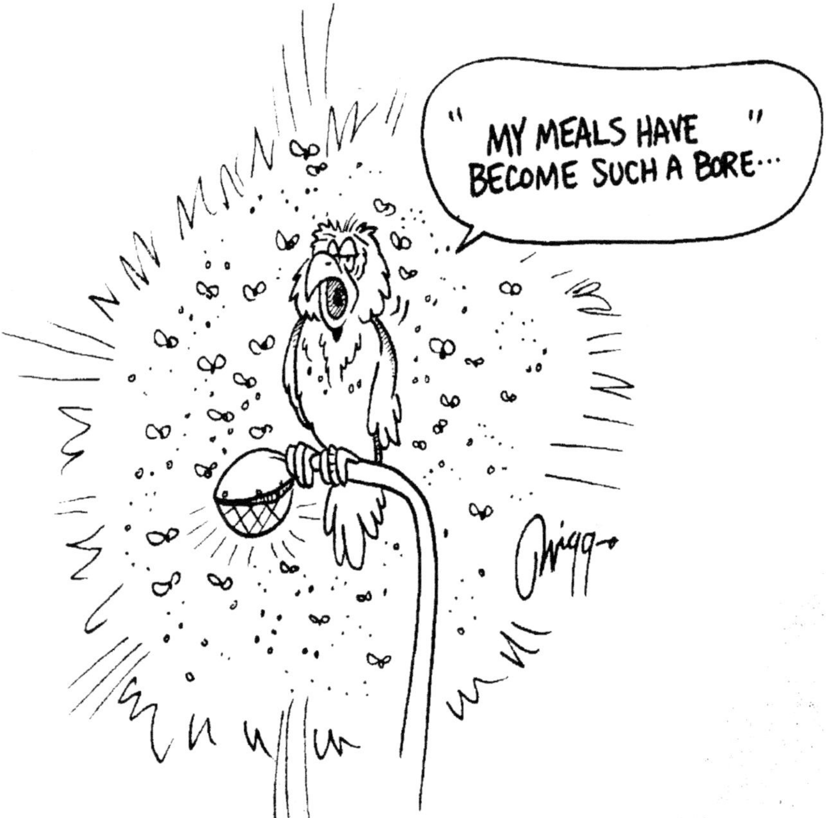
"MY MEALS HAVE BECOME SUCH A BORE..."
Quigg

Odd Duct

Deputy Game Warden Joe Shivock was cleaning his woodstove when he discovered a fish-eating duck inside. The Hooded Merganser had plunged 20 feet down his chimney, traveled across 10 feet of horizontal stovepipe and fell into the stove's heat chamber. Joe wonders if the duck was looking for a shortcut on its way south.

Call of the Wild

While towing his boat, Jeff Ceccarelli slowed for a flock of Canada geese by the roadside. But as he passed them they began flying several feet off the ground, forming a "V" pattern behind his vehicle. Apparently, the squeak coming from Jeff's boat trailer resembled a honking goose. Attracted to the sound, they chased him for several hundred feet.

Child Proof

I was standing behind a boy and his father at the post office when the youngster turned to examine my uniform. Puzzled, he looked up at his father and asked what a wildlife conservation officer does.

His Dad said, "They're the guys who try to catch people hunting deer at night." Then, with innocence typical of small children the boy shouted, "But Dad, you always hunt at night!"

Cocky!

Whenever Sarah Greenley cut grass on her riding mower a ring-necked pheasant charged from the fields, jumped in front of it and began walking backwards just inches away. The goofy bird would then ruffle its feathers and cackle vehemently in an attempt to scold the metal monster into submission.

Puppy Love

Driving along a country road, I saw a boy, his dog and a Canada goose. Curious, I asked what was up with the goose. The boy eagerly informed me that the goose, since loosing its mate, had become attached to his German shepherd. It only leaves during the molt, he explained, taking refuge in the river, then promptly returns when it can fly again. The goose has been returning to the dog for six years now!

Shock Therapy

Thinking the steady hum of electricity reverberating down a 40' pole was coming from an active beehive, a black bear climbed to the top hoping to find some honey. Instead, it touched a live wire, which sent it plummeting to the ground. It narrowly missed one of its cubs on the way down.

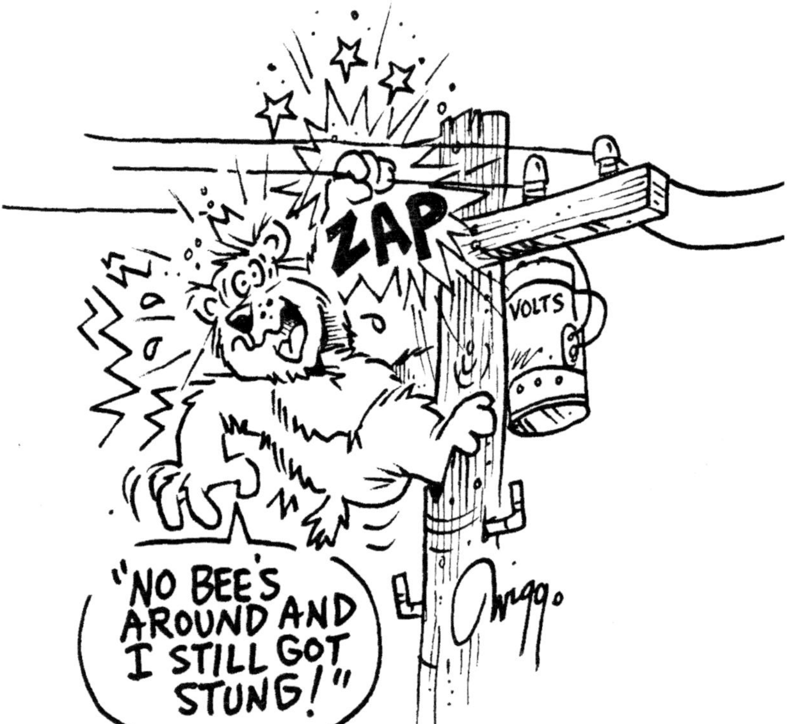
ZAP
VOLTS
"NO BEE'S AROUND AND I STILL GOT STUNG!"
Wigg.

Using One's Head

Doug Gay was walking his English setter when the dog suddenly bolted and came nose to nose with a wobbly-legged fawn. The week-old deer stood its ground, then promptly charged the dog and gave it a healthy head butt. Doug's setter quickly retreated to his side while the fawn turned and calmly disappeared in the high grass.

Supermouse

My 6-year-old daughter Sarah and I were planting flowers one day when we heard the piercing whistle of a rough-legged hawk. Gazing into the sapphire sky we watched the bird soaring on broad, flattened wings. "He's probably looking for a mouse to eat," I told my daughter.

Sarah thought for a moment, then with wide-eyed, puzzled innocence exclaimed, "But Daddy...a mouse can't fly!"

What Wildlife?

Deputy Game Warden Jeff Pierce met with a man who threatened to take a bulldozer into the beaver dam on his property and "create some wildlife habitat." Meanwhile, Jeff could see the tracks of beaver, muskrat, mink and fox along the bank; bass and sunfish were swimming nearby; frogs were croaking everywhere; and a great blue heron, waiting patiently for its afternoon meal, stood statue-like among the cattails.

Confused

A hungry coyote pounced on a local hunter using a mouth call to lure in turkeys. After realizing its mistake, the coyote quickly vanished into the brush, and the startled hunter resumed calling. But within seconds, the hunter saw the same coyote stalking him on its belly. Not wanting another wrestling match with the confused canine he jumped up, began barking like a dog, and sent the coyote scurrying to parts unknown.

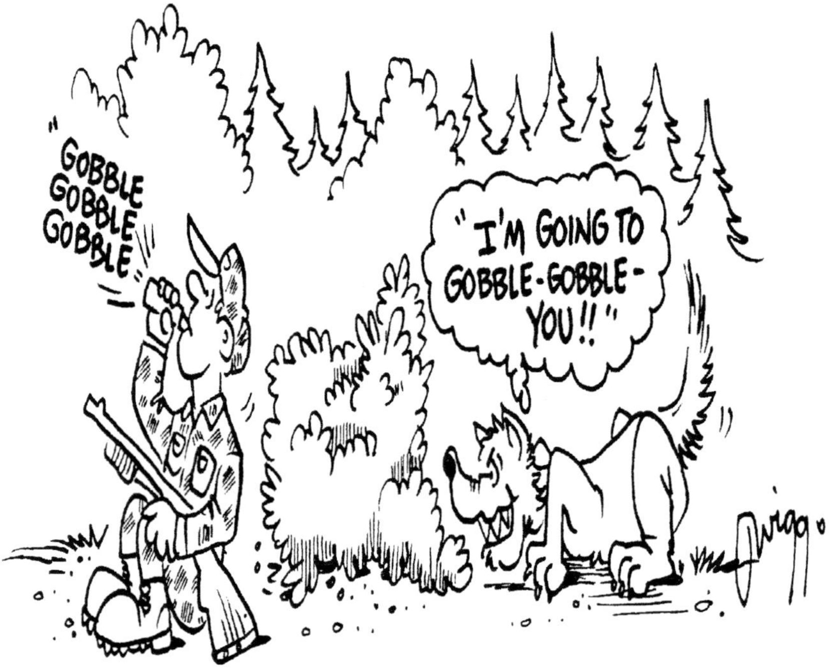
"GOBBLE
GOBBLE
GOBBLE"
"I'M GOING TO
GOBBLE-GOBBLE-
YOU!!"
Swigg

Early Bird

A teacher told me about two school-boys sent to the principal's office for fighting. The boys had been arguing over which day pheasant season started. One said it began the following Saturday because his father had asked the game warden. But the other claimed it started two days earlier because *his* father said the season always begins on the same day the game warden releases the pheasants!

Flying Fawns

Curt Bach watched as two fawns, caught in his headlights, dashed frantically to and fro until they collided into each other with such force both became airborne before collapsing. One quickly jumped up and ran off but the other just lay there.

Curt lifted the dazed fawn to its feet and walked it to the berm. At first, the whitetail refused to leave his side but after a gentle nudge the fawn scrambled off and joined its twin.

Chain Reaction

Deputy Warden Gene Gaydos was doing a wildlife program for 5th graders, when a little girl told him that a raccoon once had bitten her, and that both she and her mother had to get rabies shots. When Gene asked if the raccoon attacked her mother too, the little girl shook her head somberly, looked up at him with big blue eyes and said, "No...I bit my Mommy!"

"MY MOMMY WANTS TO KNOW IF YOU CAN RECOMMEND A GOOD TAXIDERMIST!"

Food Chain

A man I know stumbled upon an example of nature's food chain when he found the carcass of a red-tailed hawk that had collided with an electric cable. Inside the hawk's talons was a dead chipmunk...clutching an acorn.

Jail Bird

Responding to a residential burglar alarm, the police officer noticed a broken window near the front door. Stepping cautiously inside, the officer drew his gun and trained his flashlight across the room. Shattered vases and lamps were strewn helter-skelter upon tiled floors. And the culprit, a stunned and disoriented pheasant stood woodenly in one corner. The displaced bird was taken into custody and released on good behavior the following day.

Mistaken Identity

While archery hunting in camouflage clothing and sporting a new beard, Jeff Cecerrelli heard the sudden, heavy whooshing of wings. Wheeling, he was immediately struck in the chest by a red-tailed hawk. The surprised bird beat a hasty retreat while Jeff took a few minutes to regain his composure.

Jeff thinks the hawk mistook his beard for a small mammal, and although he continued to hunt that day, Jeff decided to lose the beard when he returned home.

Worrisome Worms

Deputy Game Warden Tom Scarpello got a phone call from an irate woman demanding that something be done about all the worms squirming on her driveway after a rain.

Lucky Dog

Jim Holzschuh watched in horror as a huge black bear grabbed his dog and carried it into a swamp. Grief-stricken, he chased after the bear, searching desperately for his pet. Just as he was about to give up, Jim saw his dog. It had been pushed deep into the mud with only its head sticking out. The dog's collar was badly chewed, and Jim believes it saved the dog's life by acting as a shield from the bear's teeth.

Raining Cats &
Dogs...and
Sometimes Owls

My neighbor called to complain about a screech owl living in a nearby tree. It seems that every time he walked his dog the owl would dive at him in a wild frenzy. It got so bad he had to take an umbrella along whenever he and his dog went outside.

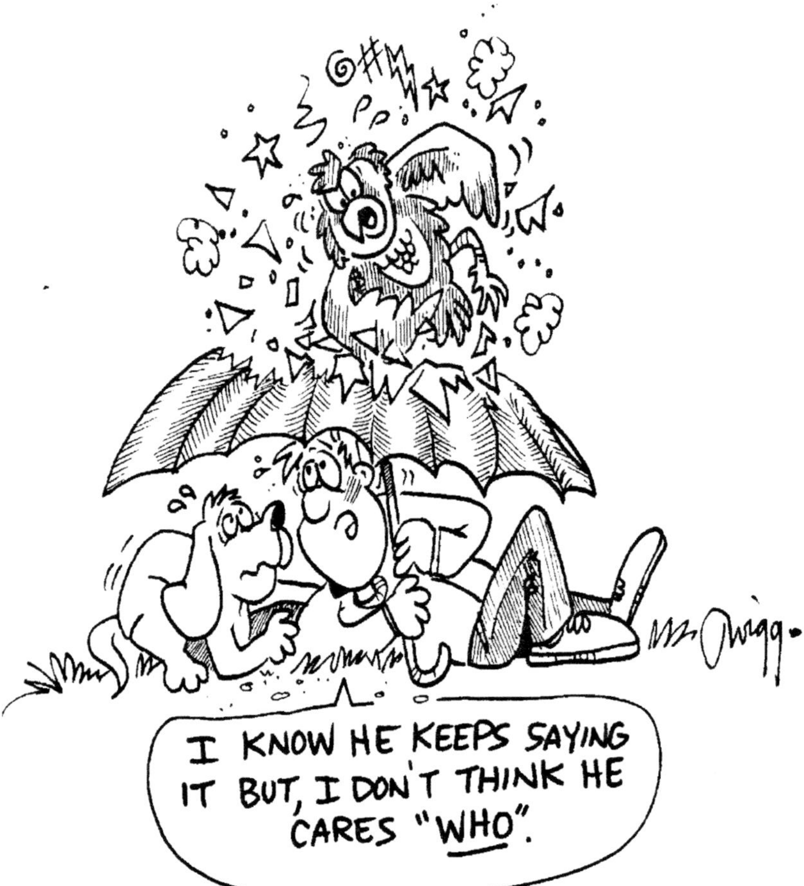
Wigg.
I KNOW HE KEEPS SAYING IT BUT, I DON'T THINK HE CARES "WHO".

The Grouse that Roared

Rod Azar told me about a wild ruffed grouse that loved to ride in the bucket of his friend's bulldozer. The grouse, named "Grumpy," would follow his friend and peck at his shoes whenever he walked about his property. One day he went turkey hunting and Grumpy tracked him down, perched on the barrel of his shotgun and bombarded him with an endless string of raspy chirps. Makes me wonder just how dumb animals really are.

Kamikaze

I watched an eastern bluebird cease flight in midair, then dive toward a large grasshopper on my lawn. But the wary insect saw the attack coming and sprang upward, launching itself into the bird's abdomen like a heat-seeking missile. The grasshopper then flew after the bewildered bluebird, chasing it into the horizon.

'Tis the Season

After decorating the classroom with colorful leaves and pumpkins to represent autumn, my daughter Sarah's kindergarten teacher asked the class what season they were in. Sarah quickly raised her hand and proudly announced, "Deer season!"

Outfoxed!

Driving along Route 6 one night, I saw a red fox standing on the berm, fixated upon dozens of lawn ornaments scattered across someone's front yard. Decorative lions, deer, fowl and a myriad of other creatures stood frozen before him in a massive ceramic army. I couldn't help but wonder what the fox was thinking. I suspect, though, that he was trying to determine whether he was about to *have* dinner or *be* dinner!

Hot Lunch

Ed Zygmunt watched in awe as an osprey dove into the Susquehanna River and snatched a bass in its talons. But as the osprey flew off, a mature bald eagle suddenly appeared. It soared just above the osprey, shadowing it until the nervous fishhawk dropped its prey. The eagle then plummeted, skimmed the water surface and arose with its booty.

On Poor Footing

I was surprised one day to see a rabbit caught in an open field dart about frantically as a large crow swooped and dove after it. But try as it may, without talons to grasp its prey like hawks and owls have, the crow simply could not capture the rabbit. Eventually they went their separate ways: the crow seeking easier table fare and the rabbit seeking better cover.

Predictable

When Deputy Warden Gene Gaydos retrieved a ruffed grouse that had crashed through a window into a family room, the woman said it was the fourth time a grouse had broken the same window, and asked why he thought this was happening. Gene, noticing the pool table and assorted board games, told her probably because the grouse was trying to perfect its reputation of being a *game* bird!

Goose Bumps

The supervisor of a manufacturing plant called me for help with a Canada goose that was attacking his employees. The crazy honker wouldn't bother anyone on foot but for some reason, it ambushed anyone on a bicycle. Luckily, most of the bikers were wearing helmets because the goose dove right at their heads.

Payback

Birds eat insects; it's not supposed to be the other way around. So, imagine my surprise when I discovered a tiny wren captured by a large preying mantis. The voracious insect hung from a twig by its hind legs while its spiny forelegs held the frantic bird in a viselike grip. Eventually the wren escaped and flittered a safe distance away.

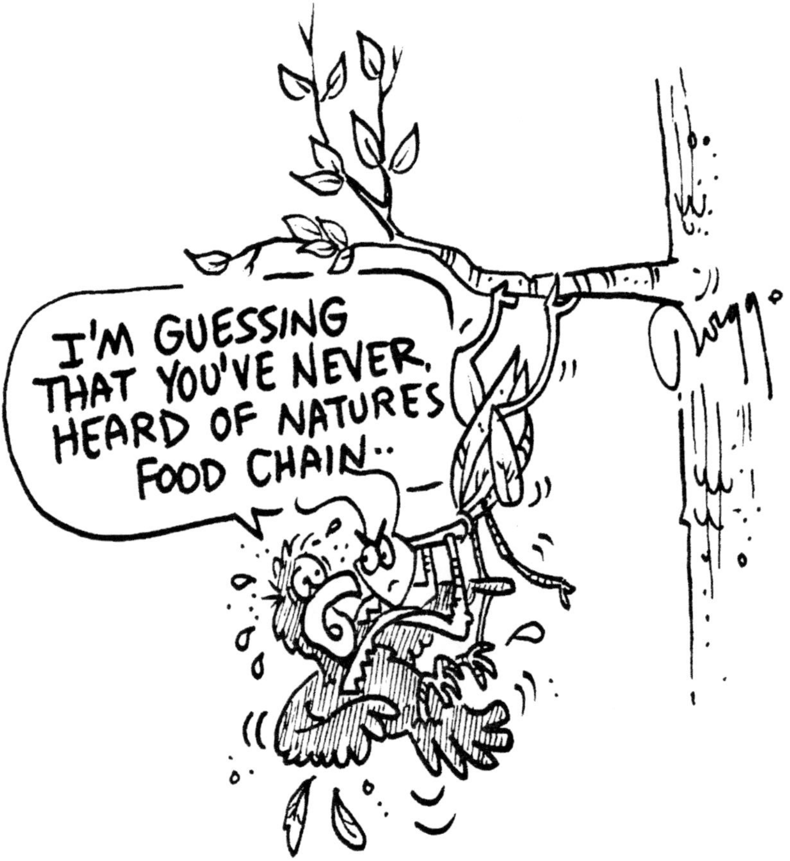
I'M GUESSING THAT YOU'VE NEVER HEARD OF NATURES FOOD CHAIN..

Unbearable

Every evening Charlie Dilione opened the lid on the dumpster behind his restaurant so a three- hundred pound black bear could pilfer food scraps. But one night Charlie forgot, and the bear climbed up on the dumpster and tried to pry open the lid while standing on it! Eventually, the frustrated bruin jumped off and gave the dumpster a wallop knocking it several feet backwards.